THIRD EDITION

THE Injured Worker's SURVIVAL GUIDE

A Worker's Guide to Alabama Workers' Compensation Cases

Five Mistakes That Can Wreck Your Workers' Compensation Claim

Tracy W. Cary, Esq.

Alabama Personal Injury Lawyers, LLC

www.AlabamaPersonalInjuryLawyers.com

Printed in the United States of America

ISBN: 978-1-63385-469-7

Design and Printing:

Word Association Publishers
205 Fifth Avenue
Tarentum, Pennsylvania 15084
wordassociation.com
1-800-827-7903

Contents

Introduction

"It's hard to beat a person who never gives up." – Babe Ruth

"I'm a greater believer in luck, and I find the harder I work the more I have of it." – Thomas Jefferson.

This book is dedicated to hard working Alabamians. Unfortunately, too many of our hard workers end up getting hurt on the job. This book is designed to help you understand your rights if that happens to you.

Alabama is home to more than five million people, including some of the hardest working people one can find anywhere in the world. Alabama's workers should expect they will be treated fairly and if they are unfortunate enough to be injured on the job, they absolutely deserve fair treatment under the law. Unfortunately though, when hard working people are injured at work, they are faced with an uphill battle against a complicated, unfair and confusing system.

Alabama's first workers' compensation act took effect on January 1, 1920. When the Alabama Legislature created the Alabama Workers' Compensation Act, they intended for the law to have beneficent (meaning generous or good) purposes. This means the Act was meant to be a good thing for injured workers and it was intended to provide good benefits for them. However, when it comes to applying the law to a particular injured worker's situation, the Act's beneficent purposes are sometimes difficult to see. The legislature attempted to strike a compromise between providing a safety net for workers who are injured on the job while at the same time addressing the concerns of industry in this State regarding the financial burdens involved in providing benefits for injured workers. Sadly, the result is that the scales seem to tilt in favor of the powerful interests of the employers and their insurance companies and against injured workers. If the law leans one way or the other, it generally leans in the favor of the rich and powerful interests and not in favor of the injured worker.

An experienced, hard working, knowledgeable and ethical workers' compensation attorney can guide you through the maze of the Alabama Workers' Compensation Act and help

Make sure you get the help you need and make sure you are treated fairly, or at least as fairly as the law allows.

Tracy W. Cary
Alabama Workers' Compensation Attorney
www.AlabamaPersonalInjuryLawyers.com
www.BamaComp.com

Foreword

Why Did I Write This Book?

I originally wrote this book intending to help injured workers and their families understand their rights and responsibilities so they could protect their jobs and their livelihood and also get fair treatment if they were unfortunate enough to be injured on the job. After practicing law for nearly 30 years, I have seen many injured workers who were not treated fairly simply because they did not understand their legal rights and all too often they were taken advantage of by more experienced or even sometimes unscrupulous insurance claims adjusters and employer representatives.

Some injured workers make the mistake of trying to go it alone. There is a reason that employers and their insurance companies never do this. They always "lawyer up" and when injured workers handle their own cases, they often get victimized twice. The latest edition of this book is a further attempt to help injured workers avoid some of the mistakes that can hurt their workers' compensation claims and have adverse effects on their lives and those of their families. It is my goal to make sure you get treated fairly. Even if you don't let me help you with your situation, I want injured workers in Alabama to have a basic understanding of their rights in a clear and understandable format.

Perhaps you have started in your search for an attorney, but you have found that so much of the attorney advertisements don't really give you that much useful information about *how to find the right lawyer* for your case. Every single one of the lawyer ads say, "hire me, we don't charge a fee unless we get you money," but then you realize that ALL personal injury/workers' compensation lawyers' ads promise that. You soon realize that claims of "We Are Aggressive" or "We Are There for You" are somewhat meaningless. (I mean, don't you have a right to expect and in fact demand that your attorney will care for you and your rights? I say you do.)

I wrote this book for **you** so that you could have some information in the quiet of your own home BEFORE you hire a lawyer and before you talk to the insurance adjuster. (Hopefully, you haven't signed insurance carrier forms yet!) The truth is that you may not even need a lawyer to pursue your claim for you. Maybe this book will give you enough information that you can pursue your rights with more knowledge than you would have had otherwise. If that's the case, then I am glad. Many injured workers are much better off by obtaining legal advice from a competent attorney. Do you really think your employer or their insurance company aren't benefitting from the advice of a lawyer? They are! And some of them feel that if that arrangement works out to your disadvantage, well then that's just the way it is.

Why should you listen to me? First, I am a worker too. I got my first job at age fourteen and worked as many as three jobs at the same time to put myself through college and law school. I have been the newest and youngest employee on the job and I have been the boss. I understand how hard our workers are working every day to provide and care for themselves and for their families. Also, I am proud to have served our country and state as an officer on active duty in the United States Army and later in the Alabama Army National Guard. I graduated from the University of Florida College of Journalism and Communications and the University of Alabama School of Law, both highly rated and nationally ranked programs. During law school I worked as a law clerk for the General Counsel in the University of Alabama Office of Counsel. After I graduated from law school, I worked as a law clerk and staff attorney at the Alabama Supreme Court for the most senior justice on the Court. Following my work at the Supreme Court, I began representing injured workers and I am proud that

I have never represented employers or their insurance carriers. My perspective comes from being a worker and then representing workers. I have been engaged in this calling since 1994.

I have taken many workers' compensation cases to trial. In full disclosure, I have lost two or three. But I have won more than 95% of the cases I have taken. In addition, I have pursued workers' compensation cases all the way to the highest court in the state -- the Alabama Supreme Court. I stood in front of the nine justices of that Court and presented my client's case with all the preparation and passion that have. I have published articles on workers' compensation in statewide magazines and have been asked to speak at numerous lawyer seminars on the issue of workers' compensation law. I have served in leadership roles of two statewide lawyer workers' compensation groups: the Workers' Compensation Section of the Alabama State Bar and the Alabama Association for Justice Workers' Compensation Section. I have been a member of a national group, the Workers Injury Law & Advocacy Group (WILG). I have represented injured workers in about two-thirds of Alabama's 67 counties. For nearly 30 years, I have worked for injured workers with a variety of different job-related accidents and situations. Each case has unique facts and issues and my staff and I work very hard to make sure the issues are developed and presented in a way that is most favorable to the injured worker. Recently a defense attorney who was on the other side of a case I was handling for one of my clients paid me what I considered to be the highest possible compliment when he said, "It's obvious to me that you care about your clients." Of course I do. I'm glad he recognized it.

My law firm, Alabama Personal Injury Lawyers, LLC, is not a general practice law firm. We don't do everything. We have made a conscious decision to specialize in just a few areas. We do not handle divorces, wills, estates, real estate transactions, criminal cases or bankruptcy cases. Instead, we focus on just a few major practice areas: workers' compensation and job-related injuries, personal injury claims such as car wrecks, truck wrecks, motorcycle wrecks, dog bites and slip and fall cases. If you need help with a legal matter outside our areas of practice, we will be glad to assist you in locating ethical and qualified legal representation. Our firm does a very limited amount of advertising because we are not a mill like some others you have seen where people become nothing more than a faceless file number. We work hard using a team approach to achieve a resolution of our clients' legal disputes in a manner most fair and favorable to our clients. Review my website, www.bamacomp.com or my firm website, www.AlabamaPersonalInjuryLawyers.com or call me at 1-205-855-2745 to schedule an appointment to discuss the specifics of your situation.

DISCLAIMER

This Book is Not Legal Advice

I must begin this book with a short legal disclaimer. This book is not legal advice. Although I provide a general overview of Alabama workers' compensation law, every case is different and it is not possible in this format to provide a comprehensive discussion of every legal issue that may be present in your case. I am not your lawyer until you and I enter into a written agreement for me to be your lawyer. That is a rule of the Alabama State Bar. Instead, my goal in writing this book is to provide you with basic information and to help you understand some common pitfalls and issues to watch out for. ***This book is not a substitute for meeting and discussing your case with a competent and qualified workers' compensation attorney.*** I strongly encourage you to seek legal counsel as soon as possible if you have been injured at work. Nothing in this book should be construed as being legal advice.

Chapter 1

Some Myths you May Have Heard from Co-Workers, Relatives, Friends and Neighbors

I have heard each one of the following myths from injured workers I have represented:

- **Myth**: My employer likes me so if I can just get a chance to talk to the insurance company or write a letter explaining my situation, I'm sure I will get a reasonable offer that "pays" me what I deserve.

- **Myth**: My cousin got a big settlement after he was injured at work and I was hurt worse than he was so my case should be worth a lot more than his.

- **Myth:** If I am involved in a work-related accident and the insurance company calls me to ask me for a statement, I have to give them a statement or they will be allowed to cut off my benefits.

- **Myth:** Every lawyer who advertises that he or she handles workers' compensation cases has the same ability, tools and experience to handle my case.

- **Myth**: My employer likes me so my employer's insurance company will quickly approve and pay for medical treatment because after all I was injured while working for my employer.

- **Myth:** My employer or their insurance company will step in and protect my rights and make sure I get the benefits I am entitled to.

- **Myth**: The paperwork I need to file is simple and the law is easy to understand.

- **Myth**: A large percentage of workers' compensation claims are just made up or fraudulent and people would rather be on compensation and "milk" the system instead of working.

- **Myth**: My employer will make sure I get the benefits I deserve quickly and keep they will keep my job open for my return.

- **Myth**: My employer will file a claim on my behalf and I will not have to do anything; notifying my employer is all I have to do.

- **Myth**: I will end up with less money if I have to pay a lawyer to represent me.

- **Myth**: I will be treated fairly by the doctor the insurance company selects and the doctor won't be influenced by the fact that my employer's insurance company is paying for my treatment.

Chapter 2

Do I *Really* Need a Lawyer's Help?

You don't need an attorney for *every* case. In fact, we may not accept your case and we may advise you to proceed on your own. Why would we do that? Because sometimes the system actually works and pays the benefits you are entitled to as an injured worker. But be careful not to be fooled by promises that an attorney makes that she or he will get you what you deserve. Unfortunately, pain and suffering is not a part of a workers' compensation case (unlike a lawsuit before a jury in other types of personal injury cases). An experienced attorney can evaluate and assess your claim, and make sure you get the maximum benefit that you are be entitled to.

Chapter 3

Finding a Qualified Workers' Compensation Attorney

Maybe you've decided you would like to talk to a lawyer but you feel intimidated by the decision of choosing an attorney to represent you. The Internet, television and radio are filled with ads that all say the same thing. Anyone can produce a slick commercial or create a website but you should not hire based solely on advertising. How do you find out who in your local community is the best for your case? There are certain questions to ask that will lead you to the best person for your case – no matter what type of claim you have. Sure it will involve some time on your part, but that's okay because the decision you are making may be critical to the success of your case. In my opinion, the world of workers' compensation is much too complex to trust your case to someone who does not handle these cases regularly. Too many times we have been called in to help people after they have talked to their doctors or after their cases have been handled by general practitioners, criminal defense lawyers, family law lawyers or commercial lawyers. Those who work within the system often refer to these types of attorneys as "tourists." But wouldn't it be better for you to hire someone who is regularly engaged in assessing workers' compensation cases?

Chapter 4

What Exactly is Workers' Compensation?

Workers' compensation is a creation of the Alabama legislature which is designed to provide certain benefits to injured workers for job-related injuries. When a worker is injured on the job and qualifies for workers' compensation benefits, the workers' compensation law almost always provides the exclusive remedy. In other words, in just about every case when you are injured on the job, workers' compensation benefits are the only thing you can pursue, whether you like it or not. In addition, the employer is almost always given immunity from any other claims that you might want to bring other than a workers' compensation claim.

Alabama law provides for a limited recovery for job-related accidents. For example, there is no compensation for pain and suffering, interference with relationships or hobbies or other types of recoveries that are possible in other personal injury actions. For that reason, it is critical to have an experienced workers' compensation lawyer review the facts of your case and serve as your advocate. Because the law is so limited, it is very important that you get the best recovery you can get.

There are a few exceptions to the exclusivity of workers' compensation law and an experienced workers' compensation attorney can advise you if your situation falls within any exceptions.

For example, if you are injured due to a defective product at work, if you are injured due to a co-worker's misconduct, if you are injured because a safety device was never installed, or not maintained or removed from a machine at work, or if you are injured in an automobile accident that takes place during your work hours, you can pursue a personal injury claim AND you can pursue a workers' compensation claim. However, the workers' compensation carrier is typically reimbursed out of your "third party" recovery for any medical expenses or benefits paid under the Workers' Compensation Act. We can advise you whether you have such a case because on a day-to-day basis we represent clients in each of those types of personal injury cases as well.

Chapter 5

Does the Alabama Workers' Compensation Act Apply to My Employer?

The Workers' Compensation Act applies to almost every employer in Alabama. Ala. Code § 25-5-50 provides that in general employers with five or more employees must either obtain workers' compensation insurance coverage or they may elect to be self-insured. The workers' compensation benefits for an injured employee are not supposed to make a difference if the employer is insured or self-insured. Several classes of employees are excluded and not covered by the Act: state employees, federal employees, railroad employees, farm laborers, domestic employees, municipalities with a population of less than 2,000 and others. Some employers who are not required to be covered may nonetheless elect to be covered. Ala. Code § 25-5-50(b).

Chapter 6

What Types of Injuries are Covered by the Alabama Workers' Compensation Act?

In simple terms, there are two types of injuries covered by the Alabama Workers' Compensation Act: injuries caused by sudden accidents and injuries that develop gradually over a period of time. It is usually not difficult to know when an injury results from a sudden accident. For example, if you are lifting something heavy at work and you experience back pain while lifting the object, you would probably know about the injury immediately. You could go to the calendar and point to a specific date and say, "that's the day I hurt my back." Other types of injuries take place gradually or cumulatively over a period of time and they can present more difficult circumstances. Sometimes workers develop carpal tunnel syndrome from repetitive motion at work. Sometimes strokes and heart attacks can be treated under the workers' compensation law. Physical injuries that result in a psychological component such as depression, anxiety or post-traumatic stress can be compensable under the law. Sadly, sometimes workers suffer fatal injuries on the job and the law provides certain benefits for the dependents in those cases.

Chapter 7

So What are My Rights Under the Law?

When you are injured on the job, you need to notify your employer as soon as possible. The law requires written notice within five days for sudden accidental injuries. The Courts modified that and said that as long as you tell a supervisor about your accident with some specificity, you are entitled to certain benefits. First, your employer or insurance carrier has an obligation to select an authorized doctor to treat you and your employer or their insurance carrier must pay for the medical bills associated with authorized treatment. What if you don't like the doctor they tell you to see? If you need treatment and you are dissatisfied with the authorized doctor, you can request a panel of four physicians. The panel of four gives you a limited ability to have some say so about which doctor treats you. Your employer or their insurance carrier must pay for any prescriptions written by authorized providers and the doctors or pharmacists are not allowed to bill you for the doctor bills or prescriptions. Also, your mileage back and forth to medical providers is reimbursed at the State's rate. When an authorized doctor takes you out of work and you miss enough work, (there is a three-day waiting period), you are paid workers' compensation benefits known as temporary total disability (TTD) benefits. These benefits are subject to a cap that increases on July 1st of each year and the benefits are calculated based on your average weekly earnings. In general, your average weekly earnings are defined as the gross pay (before taxes) that you were paid in the 52 weeks before the date of your injury. In some cases, the value of certain fringe benefits is also included in the calculation of your average weekly earnings. Your attorney will help you determine if the adjuster is calculating your average weekly wage and your TTD rate correctly.

Chapter 8

How Long Can I Receive Workers' Compensation Benefits?

You will receive TTD benefits for as long as your treatment continues until you reach maximum medical improvement or until you are allowed to return to work and paid the same rate of pay as you earned before your accident.

Chapter 9

How Long Can I Receive Medical Treatment?

Probably the most valuable benefit to injured workers under the Workers' Compensation Act is the right to receive future medical care for the rest of your life as long as you are treated for the job-related condition by an authorized medical provider and as long as you need treatment. Because this arrangement presents an unknown and potentially very expensive risk to the insurance carrier, most insurance carriers will at some point attempt to entice you to close your right to future treatment by having you consider a settlement of your right to future medical benefits. However, you cannot be forced into closing your right to future medical benefits. In other words, they cannot force you to close your future medical benefits.

Chapter 10

What is the Deadline for Filing a Workers' Compensation Claim?

Ala. Code § 25-5-80 sets forth the legal deadline or statute of limitations applicable in a workers' compensation case. The statute of limitations or legal deadline for Alabama workers' compensation claims is the latter of two years from the date of the accident or two years from the last workers' compensation benefit paid to you. Within the two-year period of time, you must either settle your case or file a lawsuit and if you do not, the law bars you from pursuing the case. For non-accidental injuries (for example, carpal tunnel syndrome that develops over time or certain breathing problems that result from exposures at work), the statute of limitations can be two years from the date you were last exposed to a condition that made the problem worse (this is sometimes known as the date of "last injurious exposure").

Once a lawsuit is filed in your case, the statute of limitations is tolled. That is to say, the clock stops ticking when you file suit. However, even if an injured worker allows the statute of limitations to run, it has no effect on the employee's right to future medical care, as long as the worker is able to prove legal and medical causation.

Chapter 11

What Are My Responsibilities If I Get Hurt on the Job?

Ala. Code § 25-5-78 provides that an injured employee must give the employer notice within five days of the occurrence of the job-related injury. The Act requires written notice but Alabama courts have said that written notice is not required if the employer had *actual notice* of the injury. Notice of the injury must be given to a supervisor, not just to a co-worker, and once the worker gives notice, the employer is obligated to provide access to immediate medical diagnosis and to facilitate the earliest possible investigation of the facts surrounding the injury. Failure to give timely notice may result in a claim being barred.

Even though Ala. Code § 25-5-78 requires notice within five days, the law contains a "savings clause" which provides that no compensation shall be payable unless written notice is given within 90 days after the occurrence of the accident. The employee bears the burden to prove that the injury was caused by, or connected with, work. Alabama cases suggest that the "arising out of" aspect relates to the causal connection between the injury and the type of employment. Alabama courts define "in the course of employment" with reference to the time, place and circumstances of the injury. There are, of course, exceptions to this general rule. For instance, if an employee is injured while performing his job but the injury is due to his own willful misconduct or the willful misconduct of another employee, or if the injury is due to horseplay or an assault by a fellow employee or a stranger, courts have traditionally not permitted recovery. Also, accidents that take place during travel to and from work are generally not covered under the Act. However, if the employer furnishes the transportation, the employer reimburses expenses or the employee is engaged in some duty in connection to his employment at home or en route, the Act may cover the accident.

Also, note that you cannot take yourself out of work and still receive benefits. A doctor has to take you out of work. I always advise clients not to quit their jobs or give their employers an easy reason to fire them. Be sure to follow all the policies your employer has in place that require you to keep them informed about your medical treatment or any absences.

Chapter 12

When Can They Cut My Benefits Off?

Most of the time, the insurance company will stop your benefits when you reach maximum medical improvement. Maximum medical improvement is defined as a condition that has become well stabilized and is not expected to change substantially in the next 12 months, with or without treatment. The idea is that when you are through with your treatment and you have recovered as much as you can, you should be able to return to work. Thus, your TTD benefits will typically be stopped. There are, of course, many times when a worker is not physically able to return to work even after he reaches MMI. Or, even if he is able to return to work, his employer does not allow him to return to work. If that happens, you could be entitled to receive unemployment benefits. Also, for some injuries (discussed in more detail later) if you are not taken back to work you will be permitted to offer evidence of vocational disability and you will not be limited to receiving compensation only for your physical impairment.

Chapter 13

What is Maximum Medical Improvement?

The American Medical Association's "Guides to the Evaluation of Permanent Impairment" defines maximum medical improvement (MMI) as "a condition or state that is well stabilized and unlikely to change substantially in the next year, with or without medical treatment. Over time, there may be some change; however, further recovery or deterioration is not anticipated." In other words, you reach MMI when the doctor concludes you have recovered as much as you are going to recover from your injury and future treatment will not improve or change your condition. When you reach MMI, the doctor will often look to the AMA's "Guides to the Evaluation of Permanent Impairment" to determine your impairment rating. The Guides generally allow for an impairment rating to be performed based upon a diagnostic related estimate or range of motion deficit. Often, your doctor will request a functional capacity evaluation (FCE) to help determine the extent of any permanent restrictions that should be considered.

Often, a functional capacity evaluation is used to determine an individual's ability to perform physical work-related activities. The evaluation is often performed by a physical therapist based on a doctor's referral. The therapist observes the patient performing a variety of physical activities and determines the level or intensity of work that a person can safely do. FCE results can be useful in making return to work decisions after injury or illness, in job placement, in vocational counseling and in disability determination.

Be aware that those who administer FCEs believe they can determine if you give full effort during the test. If the patient gives less than maximum effort, the therapist cannot determine the reasons. Factors affecting effort include pain, fear of pain or reinjury, depression, anxiety, lack of motivation, etc. FCEs are not designed to identify these underlying factors. Accordingly, be aware of FCEs that talk about secondary gain, malingering or psychological factors without a normal psychological evaluation.

Some plaintiff's lawyers object to defendant's request for a FCE on the grounds that the statue provides that only medical doctors, surgeons and chiropractors are authorized to examine the plaintiff at the request of the defendant.

Ala. Code § 25-5-77(b). The FCE is not for treatment or diagnostic purposes but for litigation.

Chapter 14

What Happens to My Benefits If I Return to Work?

Usually your workers' compensation benefits stop after you return to work. After all, it makes sense that you won't get workers' compensation benefits plus full pay after you have returned to your job. Instead, after you reach maximum medical improvement, (except for scheduled injuries as provided in Ala. Code § 25-5-57(a)(3)), when an injured worker returns to work at a wage equal to or greater than the worker's pre-injury wage, the worker's permanent partial disability rating shall be equal to his or her physical impairment and the court shall not consider any evidence of vocational disability. But if the employee has lost his or her employment under certain circumstances within 300 weeks from the date of injury, an employee may petition a court within two years thereof for reconsideration of his or her permanent partial disability rating.

Chapter 15

What About Scheduled Injuries?

There are usually two different ways a doctor can assign an impairment rating: the doctor can assign an impairment to the body as a whole or to a particular injured body part. Generally, body as a whole injuries qualify for 300 weeks of compensation but injuries to specific body parts often have fewer weeks. Ala. Code § 25-5-57(a)(3) sets out what is referred to as "the schedule." The schedule is a list of 34 body parts or combinations of body parts with a corresponding number of weeks that a worker may be compensated for a permanent injury at work. Of course, compensation is never a dollar-for-dollar replacement of what the worker has lost. Instead, the injured worker generally receives no more than 66 ⅔ percent of his average weekly wage. Here are some examples: if a job-related accident or illness causes permanent deafness to a worker's ear, the worker is entitled to compensation for 53 weeks. When a worker loses his index finger due to an on-the-job accident, he receives compensation for 43 weeks. If a worker loses a big toe after a job-related accident, he'll receive 32 weeks' compensation, and for a missing thumb, he'll be entitled to 62 weeks of compensation. Lose an eye, you'll get 124 weeks; a leg will get you 200 weeks; an arm will get you 220 weeks and a foot 139 weeks.

Most every injured body part is considered a scheduled injury; however, injuries to the head, neck, shoulders, back, and hips are not scheduled injuries. Instead, they are referred to as injuries to the body as a whole. Whole body injuries permit the injured worker to be compensated for 300 weeks or more as opposed to the more limited weeks of compensation for scheduled body parts.

The Supreme Court held in *Ex parte Drummond Company, Inc.*, 837 So. 2d 831 (Ala. 2002), that if the effects of the loss of the member extend to other parts of the body and interfere with their efficiency, the schedule allowance for the lost member is not exclusive. Thus, in order to get outside the schedule, the issue often becomes whether a worker can prove that the injury to a scheduled body part has extended to other parts of the body or interfered with their efficiency or created debilitating pain.

Chapter 16

What Does it Mean to Be Permanently and Totally Disabled?

Permanent and total disability does not mean that a worker is absolutely helpless or has suffered a total physical disability. Instead, the test for total disability is the inability to perform one's trade and the inability to obtain other reasonably gainful employment. Permanent total disability is based on a combination of factors including the following: the severity of the injury, the extent of pain, the worker's age, educational background, work experience and rate of pay. An employee who is so injured that he or she can perform no services other than those which are so limited in quality, dependability or quantity that a reasonably stable job market for them does not exist may well be classified as totally disabled.

When workers are found to be permanently and totally disabled, they are entitled to receive 66 ⅔ percent of their average weekly wage (subject to a cap) for the rest of their lives, as long as they continue to be totally disabled.

Chapter 17

What About Surveillance?

Very frequently, insurance carriers hire expensive private investigators to conduct surveillance of injured workers. There is probably nothing more damaging to your case than when you testify about certain things that you cannot do as a result of your injury and then the insurance company's lawyer presents the court with a video prepared by a private investigator that shows you doing some of the very activities you testified you cannot do. In *Ex parte Doster Construction Co.*, 772 So. 2d 447 (Ala. 2000), the plaintiff in a workers' compensation case refused to submit to a deposition based on the employer's refusal to tell him whether a surveillance video existed. The Supreme Court quoted a Louisiana decision and stated that "If the plaintiff were to view the surveillance videotape prior to being deposed as to which physical injuries and limitations during the time period pictured in the videotape, he would be more likely, either inadvertently or deliberately, to tailor his testimony to correspond with the actions pictured in the videotape." The Court held that the defendant does not have to reveal the existence of the videotape before the plaintiff is deposed, but if the defendant plans to use the tape at trial, it must be disclosed.

The best bet is to always assume you are being watched and never do things your doctor says you cannot do.

Another area to be very careful about relates to posting on social media sites such as Facebook, Instagram, etc.. You have to assume that anything you put on sites like Facebook and Instagram will be seen by the insurance adjuster assigned to your claim. If you post it, they will see it. If what you post hurts you, they will use it against you. They would love to write you no check at all or a smaller check simply on the basis of something you posted on social media that contradicted your claims.

Chapter 18

What About Unemployment Benefits?

Suppose you are fired from your job and you are not receiving workers' compensation benefits. If you apply for unemployment compensation, the decision of the unemployment agency can be very important to whether you can prevail in a wrongful termination case. Recent decisions of the Alabama Supreme Court provide that if you apply for unemployment and you lose, it can be devastating to a wrongful termination case. The opposite can also be true, so if be sure to let your attorney know in advance if you decide to apply for unemployment compensation.

To qualify for unemployment benefits, you must show that you are available to work and able to work. This means that if you are totally disabled from working you will probably not qualify for unemployment benefits. If your employer or their insurance carrier has denied your workers' compensation claim and you are still able to work but don't have a job, unemployment benefits might help you stay afloat during the time your workers' compensation case is pending. If your claim for unemployment is denied, you have a short window of time to file an appeal. Let you attorney know the very day you get a denial letter.

Chapter 19

What is the Legal Process in Workers' Compensation Cases?

In Alabama, workers' compensation cases are decided by circuit judges and not by juries. Circuit judges are the same judges who preside over wrongful death claims, medical malpractice trials, capital murder trials and divorces. Most circuit judges have crowded dockets and workers' compensation cases typically make up a relatively small percentage of their caseloads.

A workers' compensation case starts by filing a complaint in the circuit court, along with an application for employment of attorney. The court is required to approve your choice of attorney.

After the lawsuit is filed, discovery takes place. Most of the time, discovery takes two forms: written and oral. Written discovery consists of lawyers drafting written discovery requests to be answered under oath within the period of time provided by the Alabama Rules of Civil Procedure. Often, medical records and other documents are obtained with subpoenas. However, certain information is privileged and can be protected if a prompt objection is presented. After written discovery is completed, depositions are usually conducted. Most of the time the injured worker's deposition will take place. Sometimes a representative of the employee will be deposed but this is not always necessary. If necessary, one or more doctors will be deposed. If appropriate under the facts of the case, vocational experts and other witnesses may be deposed.

After discovery is complete, the case is set for trial. Most judges schedule a relatively short amount of time for the trial of a workers' compensation case. Before trial, most cases will be mediated with either a private mediator or an ombudsman with the State of Alabama Department of Labor Workers' Compensation Division.

If the case goes to trial, careful thought must be given to the strategy and presentation of the evidence. The Alabama Rules of Evidence govern what is admissible and what is not admissible into evidence. After trial, if either side is unhappy with the result, there could be one or more appeals to the appellate courts.

The process can take six months or longer, depending on the court's docket and how hard the case is worked.

Chapter 20

Settling your Workers' Compensation Case

Alabama law allows various issues to be settled in a workers' compensation case. First, if your injury results in a permanent physical impairment, Alabama law provides a mathematical formula to calculate the value of the impairment. The court is the ultimate decider of the extent of an impairment. In addition, if an injured worker is not permitted to return to work at a wage equal to or greater than the pre-injury wage, the worker is entitled to submit evidence of vocational disability. However, even if a worker returns to work making a wage equal to or greater than his pre-injury wage and thus is not permitted to present evidence of vocational disability, he can still have a claim for vocational disability if he loses his job for certain reasons within 300 weeks of the date of his accident. Finally, the workers' compensation law provides for future medical care for the rest of the injured worker's life as long as the treatment is for the job-related injury and as long as an authorized medical provider provides it.

Each of these issues can be negotiated and settled. However, it is best to have a qualified workers' compensation lawyer review any offers to determine if they are fair and also if the settlement documents fairly reflect the agreement between the parties. When we are approached by the insurance carrier about a possible settlement, we carefully analyze each individual situation to determine if settlement is the best option for you. Rest assured that in every case we work hard to make sure that our clients understand their rights and receive the maximum benefits possible.

Chapter 21

Can My Employer Fire Me If I'm Injured on the Job?

Yes, they can. Alabama is an employment at-will state. The Alabama Supreme Court has stated that workers in an employment at-will arrangement may be terminated at any time, for any reason, including for a good reason, a bad reason or no reason at all. See, *Wal-Mart Stores, Inc. v. Smitherman*, 872 So. 2d 833 (Ala. 2003). However, the workers' compensation law, at Ala. Code § 25-5-11.1, provides for a narrow exception to that general rule, and it forbids employers from terminating an at-will employee *solely* because that employee sought workers' compensation benefits. Ala. Code § 25-5-11.1 provides: "No employee shall be terminated by an employer solely because the employee has instituted or maintained any action against the employer to recover workers' compensation benefits..." I have helped many workers with these cases.

Also, state and federal law may protect employees from discrimination regarding hiring, promotion and firing. It is beyond the scope of this book to provide an overview of employment discrimination law, but if you believe you have been the victim of discrimination on the basis of certain protected classes such as age, race, gender, national origin or disability, you should immediately contact an experienced employment law attorney for advice because many employment discrimination claims are subject to very short statutes of limitation. I can help you find such a lawyer if need be.

If you are concerned about being fired because you have pursued workers' compensation benefits, you have to think about how you will prove the termination was for retaliation. You will need to document each event and conversation to help you prove your termination was in violation of the law.

Chapter 22

Five Mistakes that can Wreck your Workers' Compensation Claim

The workers' compensation law can be very complicated. If you are injured on the job, you may discover that you have entered a legal minefield. Often, your employer begins to treat you differently when you are injured on the job, even though most job-related injuries are not because the injured worker meant to get hurt. Your employer or their insurance company knows the rules that apply to workers' compensation cases and they use their knowledge to their advantage. It's not true about every adjuster, but some insurance adjusters will actually mislead injured workers about their rights. Based on nearly 30 years of representing injured workers, I have identified the following five mistakes that can wreck your workers' compensation case. If you can avoid these five problems, you may at least begin to level the playing field.

1. Failing to Give Notice Soon Enough

Many workers have good intentions for not giving timely notice of their injury to their employer. Often, workers will not notify their employer of their job-related injury because they want to be seen as a team player or because they do not think the injury is serious at first. However, Alabama law requires you to give notice to a supervisor within five days of your accident. Notice to a friend or co-worker is not usually good enough. You generally have to notify a supervisor of your accident by giving some specifics about your accident. It may not be enough just to tell your boss, "I hurt my back lifting a trash can." Instead, it is better to tell your boss, "Yesterday morning at about 8:30 I hurt my back while lifting a garbage can on the loading dock." The idea is that you need to give your employer sufficient notice about your accident so the employer can conduct a reasonable investigation into what happened.

By failing to report the injury soon enough, you may cause your employer or insurer to begin to wonder if you hurt yourself at home or someplace other than at work. In some cases, you will still be entitled to workers' compensation benefits even if you did not give notice within five days, but the longer you wait to report the injury, the more likely the insurance company will be able to argue to a judge that you did not get injured at work. The bottom line is that you should report your injury as soon as possible after it happens so there will be no questions about when or how the injury occurred. If you seek treatment for an injury at work, you should always tell the doctor that you were injured at work if that is what happened.

2. Misrepresenting Your Medical Condition in Your Job Application

Sometimes when we apply for a job we might wonder if we will be hired if we tell the potential new employer everything regarding our previous health or medical conditions. However, if you misrepresent your physical or mental condition and later receive an injury involving that same physical or mental condition, your employer or their insurance carrier might be able to prevent you from being covered by workers' compensation for that injury, even if the new job makes the old condition worse. You should always be truthful about any prior injuries and prior medical treatment. If you get hurt on the job, your employer will get your medical records and try to use any discrepancies to attack your credibility.

But if you were not truthful about the old injury on your job application, you will experience problems in obtaining workers' compensation benefits if your employer can prove the following: (1) in the course of entering into your employment relationship with your employer, (2) your employer provided you with a written warning in bold type print, "Misrepresentations as to preexisting physical or mental conditions may void your workers' compensation benefits" (3) but you knowingly and falsely misrepresented your physical or mental condition, (4) and your misrepresentation was made in writing, and (5) your condition was aggravated or reinjured in an accident arising out of and in the course of your employment.

The good news is that no preexisting condition is deemed to exist for the purposes of workers' compensation if the employee is able to perform his duties prior to the injury. Further, if a preexisting condition is aggravated by a work-related injury, the condition is still compensable even through the accident may not have caused the same injury in a normal person. An aggravation of a preexisting condition is considered a new injury under the Alabama Workers' Compensation Act.

3. Not Cooperating with Medical Care

When you are injured on the job, your employer is obligated to select a doctor to treat you. In most cases you are required to receive treatment by the authorized treating physician and your employer or their insurance carrier will have to pay for that treatment. The authorized doctor is not allowed to bill you for authorized treatment. Your employer cannot prevent the authorized doctor from providing reasonable treatment necessary to get you back to work. If you, as the injured worker, refuse to cooperate in treatment that is designed to improve your condition and return you to work, your compensation will be cut off during the period of your refusal. The best idea is always to cooperate with your physician, even if a medical provider that you did not choose is treating you. The Alabama Workers' Compensation Act gives the employer the right to select your physician and there are just a few exceptions to that rule, including emergencies, futility, acquiescence and refusal. The best advice is to ask your employer which doctor they want you to see because when they authorize a medical provider to care for your job-related injuries, the law prevents the medical provider from trying to collect payment from you for the visits.

4. Thinking the Claims Adjuster is Your Friend

Some insurance adjusters are honest but some are not. Regardless, it would be a mistake to believe the insurance company ever loses sight of the goal of saving money for the insurance company. Some insurance companies manage workers' compensation claims by having frequent communications with the injured worker and by steering the worker to particular doctors. The claims adjuster may seem genuinely concerned about your well-being and may call you every other day to see how you're doing. The adjuster doesn't want you to get an attorney or perhaps fully understand your rights under the law. Often the adjuster will hire a case manager or nurse to attend appointments with you and make suggestions to the doctor about things that are not always in your best interest. The adjuster also will sometimes secretly hire a private investigator to follow you around and record you on video when you are not aware of it. Be aware that almost always the adjuster is not on your side.

5. Agreeing to a settlement without having a lawyer advise you whether the offer is fair and the paperwork says what you want it to say.

There are generally three areas in a workers' compensation claim that could have monetary value: future medical benefits; vocational benefits; and benefits for a permanent physical impairment. Sometimes the adjuster will offer a settlement to you on one or two issues and will include the other issues in the offer without offering a higher settlement. You will be asked to sign settlement paperwork when you settle your case. Often the settlement paperwork is written in a complicated style that is not easy to understand. The best idea is to have a lawyer review the offer and the settlement paperwork to be sure the offer is fair. You don't want to sign away rights that you weren't aware you were giving up.

Chapter 23

Why Should you Hire Us?

Alabama Personal Injury Lawyers, LLC is not a general practice law firm. We focus on just a few major practice areas, including workers' compensation, motor vehicle collisions and premises liability (slip and fall cases). Unlike many large personal injury firms, our firm is small enough to offer personal attention but large enough to make sure our clients' needs are met. In addition, unlike many personal injury firms, we have extensive experience litigating workers' compensation claims in most Alabama counties.

We offer free consultations for people with questions about Alabama workers' compensation claims. Therefore, if you have been injured on the job or if you have questions about an offer of settlement or an attempt to cut off your benefits, please call or text 205-855-2745 for a free consultation or visit my firm's website www.AlabamaPersonalInjuryLawyers.com, or my workers' compensation website, www.BamaComp.com to learn more about my firm or to schedule a free initial consultation. You can also visit to get more information about our background, qualifications and practice areas. You can also email me at Tracy@AlabamaPersonalInjuryLawyers.com.

Chapter 24

What Does Our Representation of youInclude?

Keep in mind that the attorney fee is capped by the law at 15% of the recovery we get for you. You are never charged a retainer and you never get a bill for our services along the way. Every case is different and presents unique issues and challenges. However, we typically perform the following tasks for our clients in workers' compensation cases:

- Interview you and learn the unique facts of your case.
- Get a clear understanding of the concerns that you want us to address.
- Interview any witnesses necessary to pursuing your case.
- Gather all your medical records for use in your case.

- Educate you about your rights and responsibilities under the Alabama Workers' Compensation Act.
- Make sure you receive mileage reimbursement in a timely manner.
- Obtain updates after important medical procedures and visits.
- Correspond and communicate with you throughout the course of the representation so you are adequately informed about the progress of your case.
- Correspond and communicate with the adjuster so you don't have to and so the adjuster doesn't take advantage of you.
- Work with your doctor and obtain narrative reports and medical opinions about issues critical to your case.
- Obtain a copy of any video surveillance expected to be used against you at trial.
- Make sure the insurance adjuster properly calculates your weekly compensation benefit amount.
- Counsel you regarding return-to-work issues or application for unemployment benefits.

- File a lawsuit for workers' compensation benefits on your behalf.
- Work with you to answer discovery requests in a timely and ethical manner.
- Respond to subpoenas for privileged information to protect your rights.
- Prepare you for deposition at which the insurance company's lawyer will cross-examine you under oath.
- Take your doctor's deposition if necessary and cross-examine the insurance company's doctor.
- Prepare for mediation and represent you during mediation with the ombudsman program.
- Analyze any settlement proposals and work with you to determine which option is best for you.
- Prepare you for your testimony at trial.
- Represent you at the trial of your case, submit a trial brief on your behalf if necessary and cross examine opposing witnesses.
- Organize and present your medical evidence at trial.

- Consider whether to appeal your case if the result isn't favorable or oppose the appeal if the other side is the one filing an appeal.

- We continue to be available to answer questions for you and help you even after your case is over.

We are there to represent you at each step of the process. An initial consultation is free and if you hire us and we accept your claim, there is no fee unless we obtain a recovery for you. Then, our fee is capped by law at 15 percent of the recovery we get for you and is subject to court approval. We will explain each step of the process to you before proceeding and we will work with you to decide on the best course of action in your case.

Chapter 25

Ask The Lawyer Some of These Questions:

When you decide that you think you might want to hire a lawyer to fight for your rights, be sure the lawyer has sufficient experience in handling workers' compensation cases. A lot of the lawyers who advertise on television will probably never talk to you personally and they certainly will never work on your case. To help you make the decision about which lawyer to hire, ask the lawyer about these important indicators of his or her experience:

- Ask the lawyer how many years he or she has been handling workers' compensation cases. I have been representing injured workers for nearly 30 years.

- Ask the lawyer what percentage of his or her practice is devoted to handling workers' compensation cases.

Approximately 30-50% of all the cases I handle are Alabama workers' compensation cases.

- Ask the lawyer if you have to pay the expenses of litigation and court costs up front or whether the lawyer will advance those costs. We always advance the costs of litigation for our clients.

- Ask the lawyer how many workers' compensation cases he or she has taken to trial. I have tried dozens of cases.

- Ask the lawyer his or her success rate at trial. My win-loss ratio is about 99%-1%.

- Ask the lawyer if he or she is available to discuss your case. I am available to help you.

- Ask the lawyer if he or she has had any experience in handling the appeal of any workers' compensation cases. I have represented several clients when their cases got appealed.

- Ask the lawyer if he or she has argued any workers' compensation cases before the Alabama Supreme Court. I have done this.

- Ask the lawyer if the appellate courts have issued any written opinions involving workers' compensation cases for clients of his or hers. There are several written appellate decisions in cases I have handled for my clients.

- Ask the lawyer if he or she has published any articles on workers' compensation issues. I have had articles published several times.

- Ask the lawyer is he or she has authored any books on workers' compensation. I have and you are reading it.

- Ask the lawyer if he or she is available to represent injured workers across the State of Alabama. I have handled cases from Lauderdale County to Lee County, from Mobile to Montgomery, from Birmingham to Andalusia to Abbeville and from Dothan to Daleville. I pretty much cover the State.

- Ask the lawyer if he or she has served in leadership roles in lawyer workers' compensation groups. I have.

- Ask the lawyer if he or she uses technology in the practice of law to stay on top of the latest changes in the law.

- Ask the lawyer if he or she has worked with the legislature to try to get changes made in the law to benefit injured workers. The law is unfair and we constantly lobby the legislature to improve the law.

If your lawyer cannot answer "yes" to all of these questions, consider whether your lawyer has the right type of experience to handle your workers' compensation case.

We are here to help level the playing field for you. Put our experience to work for you in your important workers' compensation case.

Tracy W. Cary
Alabama Workers' Compensation Attorney

About the Author

Tracy W. Cary, Esq. is a father of four and a grandfather of five. He has traveled extensively throughout the United States and world. He earned his undergraduate degree from the University of Florida and his law degree at the University of Alabama School of Law which was recently ranked by *U.S. News and World Report* in the top 25 among all public **law** schools in the United States. Before law school, Mr. Cary received the top trainee award at basic training in the United States Army and he was commissioned as a second lieutenant in the field artillery. He then served as an officer in the Army's First Infantry Division, known as the Big Red One.

After graduating law school, Mr. Cary served as staff attorney for the senior justice on the Alabama Supreme Court in Montgomery. Then, Mr. Cary began his practice exclusively in the area of civil litigation. Since 1994, Mr. Cary has represented injured workers all across Alabama. Mr. Cary's law firm, Alabama Personal Injury Lawyers, LLC, represents injured workers in workers' compensation cases as well as other injury and accident cases.

Mr. Cary has published numerous articles in statewide magazines on workers' compensation issues and he has been invited to speak at several lawyer seminars on the issue of workers' compensation law. He has the president or chairman of two statewide lawyer workers' compensation groups and has represented injured workers in about two-thirds of Alabama's 67 counties.

Mr. Cary is licensed to practice law in Alabama, Florida, Georgia, Tennessee and the District of Columbia. He is a member of the bar of the United States Supreme Court. He has served as president of his local bar association and is an alumnus of the Alabama State Bar's Leadership Forum. For more information about workers' compensation cases, visit www.AlabamaPersonalInjuryLawyers.com or www.bamacomp.com or text or call attorney Tracy W. Cary at 1-205-855-2745 to schedule an appointment. There is no obligation and you can learn about your rights and responsibilities and that will give you some peace of mind and help you breathe easier.

I hope you found this book helpful in your search to find the right attorney.

Tracy W. Cary, Esq.

Alabama Personal Injury Lawyers, LLC

www.AlabamaPersonalInjuryLawyers.com

WA

Made in the USA
Monee, IL
04 November 2026

67381856R10046